FINDING GOD

How can we experience God?

SIX SESSIONS   **RICK RICHARDSON**

With Notes for Leaders

InterVarsity Press
Downers Grove, Illinois

These guides are dedicated to
the staff of InterVarsity Christian Fellowship
and of the Axis ministry of Willow Creek Community Church
whose hearts are big enough to want to
show and share God's love with the next generation.

InterVarsity Press
P.O. Box 1400, Downers Grove, IL 60515-1426
World Wide Web: www.ivpress.com
E-mail: mail@ivpress.com

InterVarsity Press® is the book-publishing division of InterVarsity Christian Fellowship/USA®, a student movement active on campus at hundreds of universities, colleges and schools of nursing in the United States of America, and a member movement of the International Fellowship of Evangelical Students. For information about local and regional activities, write Public Relations Dept., InterVarsity Christian Fellowship/USA, 6400 Schroeder Rd., P.O. Box 7895, Madison, WI 53707-7895, or visit the IVCF website at <www.ivcf.org>.

Scripture quotations, unless otherwise noted, are from the New Revised Standard Version of the Bible, copyright 1989 by the Division of Christian Education of the National Council of the Churches of Christ in the USA. Used by permission. All rights reserved.

Cover design: Rick Devon

Photo image: Mark Fiorenzo

ISBN 0-8308-2028-0

Printed in the United States of America ∞

P	17	16	15	14	13	12	11	10	9	8	7	6	5	4	3	2	1
Y	15	14	13	12	11	10	09	08	07	06	05	04	03	02			

CONTENTS

INTRODUCTION
HOW CAN WE EXPERIENCE GOD?

Each of us must find our own unique way to God.

Through the ages, many people have come to a fork in the road and chosen to follow God. The ways they have gotten to that point are not all that varied. In this guide, we will explore five of the different paths through which people have found God.

Some have walked the path of relationships toward God. They see the face and presence of God in the people whom they love and who love them.

Some have walked the path of nature toward God. They experience peace and a presence in the beauty of the natural world.

Still others feel they have found God through being around good people or being good people themselves.

Some have walked a path of pain. A moment of crisis, loss, hurt or unfulfilled need has driven or drawn them toward God.

Some have walked the path of facing their mortality. The experience of losing a loved one who died, or even the threat of their own death, has helped them connect to God.

We want to look at each of these paths to finding God. We want to see the strengths of each path to God but also the limitations of each path. We also want to look at the wisdom Jesus and his followers have given us about each of these paths.

Years ago, James A. Francis wrote a description of Jesus and titled it "One Solitary Life." To paraphrase one section, Jesus and his followers never held public office, never led an army, never won a war, never appeared on a talk show, never ruled a country. Yet all the armies that have ever marched, all the people that have ever ruled and even all the folk who have been guests on talk shows have not affected the world as much as the life of this one man, Jesus. What did he know about God and about life? How might Jesus be the key to finding the way to God?

In this particular guide we especially want to learn from a man whom Jesus taught. He started as Jesus' greatest enemy and became his greatest fan. His name is Paul, and his life was turned upside down when he found God. One of the intriguing things about Paul is that he thought he had already found God—until he encountered Jesus and realized how much he had missed.

Our search for God is the most important search we will ever be on. Our hope is that as you walk through these discussions, you will be helped to find God in your own way and at your own pace.

So let's see what we can learn together about how we can find and experience God.

The Groups Investigating God Series

The Groups Investigating God series was developed based on the conviction that your spiritual journey is unique and that your questions are important.

Too many of us grew up in a spiritual environment where only certain kinds of questions were valued.

These guides are especially for you if you have spiritual and life questions that you want to be able to ask and discuss and explore without fear of being judged or feeling intimidated. They are for you whether you consider yourself a skeptic or a seeker, religious or nonreligious. These guides are designed to offer help in finding spiritual wisdom for real-life issues.

What Part Does the Bible Play?

Why do we use the Bible in these discussions? Because we have found it to be a book full of wisdom for anyone who takes the time to engage with it. You don't have to "believe in the Bible" to have a great time with these discussions. You only have to be willing to see what wisdom it might shed on life's great issues.

The playing field is level. Bible passages are printed in the guide itself, so you don't have to feel intimidated by not knowing where things are.

We especially try to engage with some of the wisdom of Jesus, who was, by all accounts, one of the greatest teachers about spirituality and life who ever lived. Again, you don't need to "believe in Jesus" to get a lot out of these discussions, but just be open to the wisdom Jesus might have for your life.

How to Use These Guides

You can certainly use these guides on your own and benefit a great deal. The questions are designed to make you think, and there is space for journaling and reflection. All that you need is here. So if you want to use these guides on your own, enjoy!

At the same time, these guides are especially designed for group discussion. (A group is two or more people, so you can have a great discussion even if you are with only one other person.)

Most of us grow in life and in our spirituality as we talk and share with others. People learn best in an active mode of participation, conversation and dialogue! And we gain so much by hearing the ideas and insights of others.

If you use these guides in a group discussion format, you will need a leader. The leader will spend extra time preparing in order to help everyone get the most out of the discussion. The leader's role is not to have all the answers. Instead, the leader helps facilitate the discussion, so that everyone learns from one another and from the wisdom in the guide and in the Bible.

The leader can best help the group by using the leader's notes that are included at the end of this guide.

How to Have a Great Discussion

Here are some suggestions that will make your discussion more helpful and more fun.

1. Read over the session beforehand. If everyone gets a chance to look over the theme and some of the questions and ideas, discussion will be more rich and stimulating.

2. Remind each other of some simple guidelines that can really help the discussion go well:

a. Have fun.

b. Ask questions. Any question that is a real question for someone is a *great* question.

c. Listen to each other, and build each other up. Affirm each other whenever you feel genuine appreciation for an idea or insight.

d. Be open to spiritual growth.

e. Try to find answers from the Scripture passage when you are in that part of the discussion session. If people start going on lots of tangents, you may never get anywhere!

f. Help each other contribute but not dominate. Everyone has something to say, but no one has it all!

3. If a particular question interests you, then do some further reading and discussion with others between meetings.

The Format of Each Session

Each overall session is oriented around a question that seekers and skeptics have often asked. The introduction opens up ways different people in our culture might respond to the key question. "Going Deeper" helps us get "underneath" to uncover the real questions we have. "User's Guide" orients us to the Bible wisdom we will discuss. "The Oracle" is a Bible passage that addresses the topic. "Musing" has questions for group discussion around the Scripture and the overall theme. "Challenge" summarizes the wisdom in the Bible section and suggests what choices we may face. "God Moment" describes how someone has found freedom and personal growth. "Self-Reflection" gives you a chance to reflect on and perhaps journal about your own journey. There may also be an optional prayer you can use as you feel comfortable.

About This Series

Spiritual hunger is at an all-time high. But people are not necessarily interested in traditional ways of meeting that hunger. So some leaders from InterVarsity

Christian Fellowship and Willow Creek Community Church's Axis Ministry have created these guides as an answer to people who are spiritually interested but looking for fresh ways to explore their interest.

We are seeing an exploding movement of "Groups Investigating God"—people meeting together to have discussions like these. We hope you will benefit from these discussions as you find your way in life.

At the end of the guide, we give you other resources and help for your journey.

Rick Richardson
Series Editor

9

ONE

CAN I FIND GOD THROUGH RELATIONSHIPS?

To love and be loved is the greatest happiness of existence.

SYDNEY SMITH

In the movie *Titanic,* Rose is to marry Cal, but she feels suffocated by his world of power, privilege and lordly men. Jack Dawson, an artist who lives for the moment, falls in love with Rose and invites her to love him back. She does. And when the great ship goes down, Jack helps Rose survive, though he himself succumbs, sinking beneath the icy waters.

Later, aboard the rescue ship *Carpathia,* when asked for her name, Rose takes Jack's last name as her own. The name is a symbol of her sense of lifelong commitment to and love for this man Jack Dawson, who saved her life.

When Rose tells this story years later, she says: "I've never spoken of him until now, not to anyone, not even to my husband. A woman's heart is a deep ocean of secrets. But now you know there was a man named Jack Dawson, and that he saved me in every way that a person can be saved."

Rose dies in her sleep. But the movie's final scene shows Rose and Jack, once again aboard the *Titanic*, embracing and kissing, to the applause of all the passengers.

- ■ *What do you think of this picture of relationships?*
- ■ *Can you think of ways that relationships can save us?*
- ■ *What's unrealistic about the relationship in this picture?*

Going Deeper

A favorite text at weddings is the great poem of love by St. Paul: "Love is patient and kind. . . . It bears all things, believes all things, hopes all things, endures all things. Love never ends."

We long for a relationship that will never fail. But often life doesn't work out that way. Most of us had parents who tried to love us but sometimes failed us, and may even have scarred us deeply. Friendships may last for a while—and then fade away. Even the best of marriages have their car wrecks. And many marriages come to an end. We can feel let down or even betrayed in any relationship. As a result we can become cynical, defensive and distant.

We might wonder how long Rose and Jack would have lasted if Jack had survived the sinking of the *Titanic*.

And yet our hearts sense that we were made for relationships and that we ought to be able to see the face of God in other people. After all, aren't loving others and loving God related ideas and actions? So all the saints have said.

What do we do with this sense that relationships are important, and can even help us know God, when we are so often let down and hurt in relationships?

User's Guide

In this guide, we will be learning from the early Christian teacher, the apostle Paul. Paul was at one time the greatest opponent of Christians and the greatest enemy of Jesus. Then, on the road to a Syrian town called Damascus, he had an encounter with Jesus . . . after Jesus reportedly had died. The encounter shook him up a bit! Paul then became Christianity's greatest proponent and hero. He taught more profoundly about finding God than anyone else did, with the exception of Jesus himself.

Here are some of Paul's great thoughts on the topic of love and a relationship that won't fail. Paul, who had been so opposed to Christians, experienced the presence and love of God through Jesus. The experience marked him deeply and carried him through intense suffering and hardship. He is exuberant, but not superficial or trite, in his understanding of the power of this love.

The Oracle

[Love] bears all things, believes all things, hopes all things, endures all things. Love never ends. (1 Corinthians 13:7-8)

What then are we to say about these things? If God is for us, who is against us? He who did not withhold his own Son, but gave him up for all of us, will he not with him also give us everything else? Who will bring any charge against God's elect? It is God who justifies. Who is to condemn? It is Christ Jesus, who died, yes, who was raised, who is at the right hand of God, who indeed intercedes for us. Who will separate us from the love of Christ? Will hardship, or distress, or persecution, or famine, or nakedness, or peril, or sword? As it is written,

> "For your sake we are being killed all day long;
> we are accounted as sheep to be slaughtered."

No, in all these things we are more than conquerors through him who loved us. For I am convinced that neither death, nor life, nor angels, nor rulers, nor things present, nor things to come, nor powers, nor height, nor depth, nor anything else in all creation, will be able to separate us from the love of God in Christ Jesus our Lord. (Romans 8:31-39)

Musing

1. Paul talks about the unfailing love of God. Have you ever felt loved like this, and if so, what was that like?

2. Paul points to some evidences of God's love—things God has done to show us how much he loves us. In the first seven lines of the Romans passage, what does Paul say God does or has done to show his love? What do you think of these things?

3. There are two lists that point to things that might—but don't—separate us from God's love. When do you feel distant from God?

4. How does God's love, as talked about in this passage, compare with and contrast with human love in your experience?

5. Paul ought to feel defeated and depressed by some of the things that he has gone through, like hardship, distress, persecution and famine. How does his certainty about God's love affect his attitude in the midst of these struggles?

6. What do you think of his attitude?

7. Where in your life do you feel like you need to experience the kind of unfailing love that Paul says God has?

Challenge

Paul tells us that God loves us passionately, and that God has proven it by giving us Jesus. God has shown us, through Jesus, just what he thinks about us. Human relationships will fail us sometimes. But God never fails. God will always be our greatest advocate and our most dependable friend. God will bear all things, believe all things, hope all things and endure all things—for us!

But it can be hard to see God's love concretely in our lives. We have to trust God in order to experience God.

So we have a choice. Will we choose to trust and seek and embrace and receive that love? Or will we choose to go our own way and separate ourselves from God's love?

■ *How do you respond?*

GOD MOMENT

My Story

After a painful romantic breakup at the end of high school, I went into a shell and built a wall around myself. But I still needed to feel loved, to belong. So, starting midway through my freshman year in college, I began a series of dating relationships that were my attempt to find love, acceptance and belonging.

During those next three years of college, I had to be dating at all times. If I didn't have someone to go out with, I knew I would be unhappy, that I would have to face what I was feeling inside. So I filled the time with relationships and with escape. I escaped into fantasy (Go Trekkies!) and constant music. I escaped into the parties at my Sigma Chi fraternity house. And I was always starting a new relationship as soon as the old one ended. Sometimes in awkward ways, the beginning of a new relationship overlapped with the ending of the old one.

But all the relationships ended, leaving me feeling more empty, more in pain, than before.

Then I met and became friends with a guy named Jim. He had that deep inner sense of peace and contentment that I so longed for. He began to point me to a relationship that he claimed had never failed him, a relationship he said met the inner emptiness that he too had felt. He began to point me to a relationship with God. And I began to seek the God whom Jim seemed to know well.

14

■ *In what ways can you relate to this personal story?*

Self-Reflection

Look at the following chart, and reflect on where you are in your spiritual journey.

Skeptical	Apathetic	Curious	Actively Seeking	Feeling Connected	Following God

■ *What do you hope will happen in your life as a result of these discussions?*

■ *What have you realized about yourself in this study? Use this space to journal your thoughts.*

If you're comfortable, end with the following prayer: *God, I want a relationship that will last and will fill the inner emptiness I feel. Show me your love. And show me the way to connect with your love.*

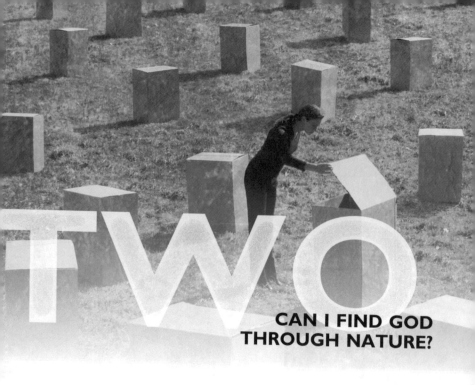

TWO

CAN I FIND GOD THROUGH NATURE?

The Force be with you!

OBI WAN KENOBI

Yet as biochemists discover more and more about the awesome complexity of life, it is apparent that the chances of it originating by accident are so minute that they can be completely ruled out.

FRED HOYLE, ASTRONOMER

In *The Empire Strikes Back*, Luke Skywalker visits the Degobas system to be mentored by Yoda in the ways of the Force. Luke has a rough landing in a misty swamp. He meets a little gerbil-like being who talks in a very odd cadence. This odd little hamster turns out to be the famed Jedi warrior Yoda. Yoda reluctantly agrees to mentor Luke. He takes Luke through a series of exercises to teach him how to use the Force.

During one exercise, Luke and Yoda are at the site of Luke's sinking starship. The ship slips beneath the surface of the swamp and disappears. Yoda tries to get

Luke to raise the ship using the Force. Yoda tells Luke about the Force: "Life creates it, makes it grow. Its energy surrounds us and binds us. Luminous beings are we, not this crude matter. You must feel the Force around you. Here, between you, me, the tree, the rock, everywhere. Even between the land, the ship." Yoda goes on to raise the ship.

Luke responds, "I can't believe it!"

Yoda replies, "That is why you fail."

Yoda teaches Luke that the Force is the consciousness of the universe, the life force that ties everyone and everything together.

■ *Yoda thinks God is "the Force," the consciousness and the ultimate life energy of the universe. Do you agree with Yoda? Do you think God is like a force, or do you think God is more like a person? Why?*

■ *What do you think it is about nature that helps people connect to God?*

Going Deeper

Some of us find God initially through nature. We are drawn to the great outdoors, and we love the majesty, beauty and harmony we find in nature. We may sense that the goodness of nature didn't happen just by chance. In nature, we experience a sense of peace that may help us connect with God. Nature is not just "there." There is something more behind and beyond it. Somebody put it there.

The Bible describes this intuition we have this way: "For since the creation of the world God's invisible qualities—God's eternal power and nature—have been clearly seen, being understood from what has been made."

But what is this God like? Is God like a force? Or a person?

User's Guide

What follows is one of Paul's earliest speeches to a group of philosophically minded people in Athens, Greece, a great center of learning and thought. Paul talks about this sense of God in nature and what we can know about God through nature.

The Oracle

Then Paul stood in front of the Areopagus and said, "Athenians, I see how extremely religious you are in every way. For as I went through the city and looked carefully at the objects of your worship, I found among them an altar with the inscription, 'To an unknown god.' What therefore you worship as unknown, this I proclaim to you. The God who made the world and everything in it, he who is Lord of heaven and earth, does not live in shrines made by human hands, nor is he served by human hands, as though he needed anything, since he himself gives to all mortals life and breath and all things. From one ancestor he made all nations to inhabit the whole earth, and he allotted the times of their existence and the boundaries of the places where they would live, so that they would search for God and perhaps grope for him and find him—though indeed he is not far from each one of us. For 'In him we live and move and have our being'; as even some of your own poets have said,

'For we too are his offspring.'

Since we are God's offspring, we ought not to think that the deity is like gold, or silver, or stone, an image formed by the art and imagination of mortals. While God has overlooked the times of ignorance, now he commands all people everywhere to repent, because he has fixed a day on which he will have the world judged in righteousness by a man whom he has appointed, and of this he has given assurance to all by raising him from the dead." (Acts 17:22-31)

Musing

1. Paul affirms how spiritual the Athenians are, but he is concerned that they are pursuing their spiritual search by worshiping artwork made of gold, silver and stone. Do you think there are ways to pursue spirituality that are unhealthy? If so, what do you think those might be?

2. Describe the picture Paul paints of God in this passage.

3. Would you say that you believe that God made the world? Why or why not?

4. What in your own life do you think strengthens a hunger to know and believe in God, and what do you think weakens that desire?

5. Paul teaches that because God made the world and established the existence and boundaries of the nations, God deserves to be worshiped and has the right to judge us. Do you agree that God has the right to lead and judge our

lives, and why or why not?

6. What difference would it make to the way you live if you believed that God had the right to lead and judge your life?

7. Paul talks about how God will have the world judged through Jesus and has proved the point by raising Jesus from the dead. What's your opinion of Paul's conviction here?

Challenge

Like Paul, many of us have sensed God in nature. But much about God is unknown if we go just by nature. The Athenians knew that they could only partly know God on their own, and so they built an altar to an unknown god. Paul claims that the times of ignorance, of God's being largely unknown, are over. Jesus has changed all that. If nature prepares our hearts to know God, Jesus leads us right into the inner reality of God. Yet many of us turn away from this picture of God.

If God made the world, established the nations, sent Jesus to help us find God and will judge us in the end, then we are accountable to God; our lives need to be lived as if God's opinions are what matter most. We don't want to be accountable in that way. And so we may be more comfortable with seeing God as a force instead of a person, so we don't have to make changes in our lives.

We have a choice. Will we seek God whatever the consequences for our lives? Or will we make God in our own image, as the Athenians did by using stone and silver and gold—a God who makes no demands and can fulfill no promises?

■ *How do you respond to this challenge?*

GOD MOMENT

Bob's Story

In my thirtieth year I came to the end of my rope. My wife had become a Christian, and frankly that scared me. I was drinking pretty heavily. I remember one night driving out to a hill near our house. I was drinking again. I felt miserable, wondered if I wanted to keep living. Gradually all that night, I drank down whiskey to numb my pain. As the sun rose that next morning, I finally began to realize how pointless and painful my life had become. At that moment, I cried out to the heavens, not at all sure if there was anything there. I cried out to a God I wasn't even sure existed. My prayer was pretty simple: "God, if you're there, and you care at all about me, show me. You just have to show me." From that moment my life began to change, slowly at first. But I would never be the same. The bottle has been gone from my life for nearly thirty years now. I've written books, taught young people, started a church and had a full life, and I'm still going strong. That one little prayer was the turning point of my life.

■ *In what ways can you relate to Bob's story?*

Self-Reflection

■ *What have you realized about yourself through this study?*

If you feel comfortable, end with the following prayer: *God, I want to seek and find you if you're really there and you really care. So, if you are there and you do care, show yourself to me, God. I need to know that you're there.*

THREE

CAN I FIND GOD BY BEING A GOOD PERSON?

If God grades on the curve, I'll make it.

A STUDENT

In the movie *Gladiator,* Maximus, a Roman general, is betrayed by Commodus, the son of the emperor. Commodus first kills his own father, the emperor, and then orders Maximus and all his family executed. Unknown to Commodus, Maximus survives, though Maximus's wife and son are killed. Maximus becomes a slave, then a gladiator. And then he captures the hearts of the people in the Great Arena in Rome. Commodus himself decides to fight Maximus in the Great Arena, in order to win back the hearts of the people. But before he does, he gives Maximus a wound in the back that will not be seen by the people but will slow him down and cause his death. Against impossible odds Maximus still wins, and with his dying breath, he frees the slaves and gives the rule of Rome back to the people.

When the battle has ended, the princess Lucilla, who has loved Maximus for many years, rushes past her dead brother Commodus to embrace Maximus before he dies. She then releases Maximus to the afterlife and to a joyous reunion with his wife and son. She lingers, weeping. When she rises, she says to all gathered: "Is Rome worth one good man's life? We believed it once. Make us believe it again. He was a soldier of Rome. Honor him."

Senator Gracus, the new leader of Rome, responds, "Who will help me carry him?" And all the great ones do.

Maximus is a true hero. He is a good man who makes Rome believe in herself again. In the final scene, he joins his wife and child in the afterlife.

■ *Do you have any heroes? If so, what are they like? If you don't have any heroes, talk about why.*

■ *In the film, Maximus is rewarded in the afterlife. Do you think people are rewarded after they die for what they do in this life? Why or why not?*

Going Deeper

Many of us believe that all God wants is for us to be pretty good people. If we mind our own business, don't hurt others very often and help out when we can, what more could God want? God is so loving and forgiving that we're sure God forgives people for the things they've done wrong. After all, most of us have never done anything seriously wrong, say, on the level of killing someone, or terrorism, or stalking, or anything like that. And even if we have, won't God let it go? After all, God is loving, right?

Today we'll discuss whether we can find God by being a fairly good person.

User's Guide

What follows is another section in Paul's literary masterpiece, the book of Romans. Paul is a realist. He explores the question of what difference it makes that God is loving when life is so messed up. And why is life so messed up? How does life get better? Paul wants to show that God's love is powerful enough to reach us even in the depths of our hurts and struggles. And the only way Paul can make a convincing case is by taking a very honest look at the dark side of the human heart. According to Paul, God takes our dark side very seriously. That's what we'll look at next.

The Oracle

For the wrath of God is revealed from heaven against all ungodliness and wickedness of those who by their wickedness suppress the truth. For what can be known about God is plain to them, because God has shown it to them. Ever since the creation of the world his eternal power and divine nature, invisible though they are, have been understood and seen through the things he has made. So they are without excuse; for though they knew God, they did not honor him as God or give thanks to him, but they became futile in their thinking, and their senseless minds were darkened. Claiming to be wise, they became fools; and they exchanged the glory of the immortal God for images resembling a mortal human being or birds or four-footed animals or reptiles.

Therefore God gave them up in the lusts of their hearts to impurity, to the degrading of their bodies among themselves, because they exchanged the truth about God for a lie and worshiped and served the creature rather than the Creator, who is blessed forever! (Romans 1:18-25)

Musing

1. Paul talks about the wrath of God. The word *wrath* means just or rightful anger. What things do you get rightfully angry about?

2. Paul says God gets rightfully angry at people who suppress the truth, who exchange the truth for a lie. What's the truth that Paul talks about in the second and third sentences? What's the lie?

3. Next Paul paints a picture of people who won't honor God and who worship created things or people. Why do you think people might choose not to honor God or give thanks and instead worship created things or people?

4. When people turn away from God, God turns away from people and gives them up to the consequences of their choices. What do you think of God's response?

5. Do you agree or disagree with Paul that people's lives become chaotic and addictive when they turn their backs on God and start to live soley according to their instincts? Why or why not?

6. So according to Paul, what's the basic human problem?

7. In what ways do you agree or disagree with Paul?

Challenge

Paul tells us that we often sense that God exists, but we don't want to honor God or give thanks because "I want to do what I want to do!" We live by our needs and feelings, not worrying about being accountable to God or about changing our patterns. We all have a "self" problem. We are addicted to self-rule, self-gratification, self-promotion. So we turn away from God. Go our own way. Run our own lives. We feel like fairly good people when we compare ourselves to other people who have done terrible things. But we need help. We need a solution to the problem of the dark side of the human heart.

We have a choice. Will we admit that we have a self problem and turn back toward God for help? Or will we choose to continue to live in a world with ourselves at the center, leaving God to the side?

■ *How do you respond?*

GOD MOMENT 25

Abner's Story

My life was empty, and my friend Alex had something I wanted. He seemed happy, like he knew what life was about. He invited me to this meeting called "The Edge." I went, and afterward, I was so mad! This guy who was speaking, named Doug, was telling me my life, reading my mail. I was so ticked at him! But afterward I told Alex, "I want to meet your friend Doug."

When I met with Doug, I went on the attack, asking if he honestly believed you could only know God through Jesus. I pointed to Gandhi and to others who had lived a good life. Doug challenged me to put Gandhi aside for a minute and look at myself. He shared how his life had been so messed up. He didn't need some ten-step plan to get to God, like many religions offer. He didn't need some way to be good enough. He needed help for his struggles and his mistakes and his pain. He needed God to come and find him. And then he looked me in the eye and said, "I think you need that too, Abner. I think you're nearly as messed up a person as I am. You don't need ten steps to find God. You need God to find you, to help you and to heal your heart. Am I right?"

Boy, did I get even madder. But I also knew in my heart he had nailed me. I told Doug I would give God three weeks to show me he was there, and Doug just smiled. And God did show up. (Abner finishes his story in session six.)

■ *In what ways can you relate?*

Self-Reflection

■ *What have you realized about yourself in this study? Where in your life do you need help with the dark side of your heart?*

If you feel comfortable, end with the following prayer: *God, I realize I have a self problem—a sin problem. I want to run my own life and leave you out of the picture. Help me turn from self-centeredness toward God-centeredness. Help me with my heart.*

CAN I FIND GOD THROUGH MY PAIN?

Pain is God's megaphone to rouse a deaf world.

C. S. LEWIS

In the movie *The Devil's Advocate*, Al Pacino plays the role of the devil, and Keanu Reeves plays Kevin, his successful lawyer son. The devil drives Kevin's wife, MaryAnn, to suicide, and then Kevin confronts the devil (who he doesn't know is his father) in intense pain and anguish. Kevin cries out, asking what happened. Why did his wife have to die?

The devil presses Kevin, intensely cross-examining him to show Kevin it was his own fault, his choice. He had been too busy winning cases to pay any attention to MaryAnn. The devil reminds Kevin that he had told him, "Maybe it was your time to lose." Kevin responds: "Lose? I don't lose. I win. I win. I'm a lawyer. That's my job. That's what I do."

The devil retorts, "I rest my case. Vanity is definitely my favorite sin. So basic. Self-love. The all-natural opiate. It's not that you didn't care for MaryAnn, Kevin. It's just that you were more involved with somebody else—yourself."

Then guilt hits Kevin. The devil doesn't want guilt because he knows guilt might lead to taking responsibility and turning toward God. So the devil compares carrying guilt to carrying bricks and asks, "Who are you carrying all those bricks for? God? Let me give you some inside information about God. God likes to watch. He's a prankster. Think about it. He gives man instincts. He gives you this extraordinary gift, and then what does he do? I swear for his own amusement, his own private gag reel, he sets the rules in opposition. It's the goof of all time. Look, but don't touch. Touch, but don't taste. Taste, but don't swallow. And while you're jumping from one foot to the next, what is he doing? . . . He's an absentee landlord."

Kevin muses, "Better to reign in hell than serve in heaven. Is that it?"

The devil responds: "Why not? I'm here on the ground with my nose in it since the whole thing began. I've nurtured every sensation man has been inspired to have. I cared about what he wanted, and I never judged him. Why? Because I never rejected him. In spite of all his imperfections, I'm a fan of man. I'm a humanist. Maybe the last humanist. Who in their right mind, Kevin, can possibly deny that the twentieth century was entirely mine? All of it. Mine. I'm peaking. It's my time now. Our time."

■ *Kevin is in anguish, but he realizes his pain is self-inflicted. Do you think most pain in our lives comes from our own choices, or do you think most pain comes from things beyond our control? Talk about your response.*

■ *What do you think of the picture of God in this scene?*

Going Deeper

Have you ever suffered or been hurt? Are you hurting now? Suffering and pain can make us feel abandoned by God or even drive us to question whether there is a God. And yet, suffering also pushes us to look beyond ourselves for help. It is often in times of pain that people find God.

Some of us have experienced a painful breakup. Others grew up in families that didn't love well. Maybe we experienced abuse, abandonment or indifference from the people we wanted to trust. Some of us are caught in addictive patterns that cause us a lot of personal pain and shame.

Jesus suffered too, and not as the consequence of his own poor choices. Why did Jesus, a truly innocent man, have to suffer so much? Why do bad things happen to good people?

In this study we will discuss Jesus' suffering, and we'll see how what Jesus went through can help us in our times of pain.

User's Guide

This next writing from Paul is so rich and deep that it will be a challenge to understand it. But it is at the heart of Paul's insights into how to find God. It talks about what the pain and suffering of Jesus meant. Because Jesus is God and has suffered, we can go to God with our pain and find an understanding and compassionate heart. What's even more powerful is that the suffering of Jesus helped the whole world. There is profound meaning in suffering. Jesus' suffering gives us life and hope in our own suffering.

The Oracle

For the love of Christ urges us on, because we are convinced that one has died for all; therefore all have died. And he died for all, so that those who live might live no longer for themselves, but for him who died and was raised for them.

From now on, therefore, we regard no one from a human point of view; even though we once knew Christ from a human point of view, we know him no longer that way. So if anyone is in Christ, there is a new creation; everything old has passed away; see, everything has become new! All this is from God, who reconciled us to himself through Christ, and has given us the ministry of reconciliation; that is, in Christ God was reconciling the world to himself, not counting their trespasses against them, and entrusting the message of reconciliation to us. So we are ambassadors for Christ, since God is making his appeal through us; we entreat you on behalf of Christ, be reconciled to God. For our sake he made him to be sin who knew no sin, so that in him we might become the righteousness of God. (2 Corinthians 5:14-21)

"My God, my God, why have you forsaken me?" (Jesus' cry from the cross, Mark 15:34)

Musing

1. What are the benefits of being reconciled with God? (See lines 4-7 of the Oracle.)

2. Why do you think Jesus felt so abandoned by God on the cross? (As you answer, think about what the last couple of lines of the 2 Corinthians 5 passage might mean.)

3. How might it help you when you face pain to know that during his life Jesus suffered for us?

4. This passage points to a great exchange. Jesus took our death and sin on himself and gave us his life. We are now new creations and get a fresh start. In what areas of your life would you like a fresh start?

5. If you knew you had the power to make new choices and live this new life, what are some things you would do differently?

Challenge

Our choice to run our own lives, to pursue self-rule, self-gratification and self-promotion, ends in spiritual death and separation from God. But God, out of his great love for us, sent his Son to die a painful death on the cross and to experience the separation from God that we deserve. If we accept Jesus' death in our place, we are given a new life. We become "a new creation"; we get a fresh start. God's rightful anger against sin and self-centeredness is resolved at the cross, and God is free to become one with us through Christ, with no barrier, hindrance or reserve. We can be reconciled to God! And we can then begin to live in his immense, passionate and practical love.

So we have a choice. Will we humbly accept the death of Jesus in our place, admitting that we needed him to take the pain of spiritual death that we deserved? Will we accept Jesus' way of getting a fresh start? Or will we hang on to our old life and try to do it on our own?

■ *How do you respond to this challenge?*

GOD MOMENT

Vicki's Story

I'm from an Asian American family. I believe my parents loved me, and they were very responsible in providing for me. But I always felt like I didn't "measure up" in my mom's eyes. I always felt like she was looking at me and noticing every single thing I didn't do quite right. And I felt my dad was distant. I couldn't connect.

In college, my struggles came to a head. I was living with a person who led a weekly Bible study, but who was full of pain and neediness too. We shared our struggles; we shared our clothes; we shared everything, until finally we shared our bed. I entered a six-year journey in the lesbian community.

At first, I felt like my pain was lessened by my sexual and emotional involvements. But with each painful breakup I felt emptier, more alone and more lost. My parents were devastated and wouldn't speak to me because of my lifestyle choices. They just felt shame. In a way I felt okay about my separation from my parents, because it got me out of those situations where I felt Mom's criticism and Dad's distance.

Then I met a man who had been in the gay lifestyle but had experienced a lot of healing. He began to talk about the suffering God. My heart began to melt toward Jesus as I came to understand his suffering and aloneness and pain at the time of his death. And my friend shared the power of Jesus' death to bring forgiveness and healing into my life.

I joined my friend's church community and began to walk in the way of healing. I won't say it wasn't hard. But I can say now, five years later, that the suffering of Jesus became the key to healing and forgiveness for me. I have since left the lesbian lifestyle, married and reconciled with my parents. I still struggle at times with loneliness and feelings of being abandoned. But I know now where I can find compassion and a presence when I hurt.

■ *In what ways can you relate? Where in your life do you need the kind of comfort and hope Vicki found?*

Self-Reflection

■ *What have you realized about yourself in this study? Where do you need the comforting and healing presence of God in your life?*

If you're comfortable, end with the following prayer: *God, I bring my pain to you. I thank you that your pain and suffering on the cross mean I can be reconciled to you and become a new person. I admit that I have tried to run my own life. Jesus, I accept your death for me. God, give me a fresh start. God, be my forgiver and my leader.*

FIVE

WILL I FIND GOD IN LIFE AFTER DEATH?

Frisbeetarianism is the belief that when you die,
your soul goes up on the roof and gets stuck.
GEORGE CARLIN

In *The Matrix,* Neo is recruited by a woman named Trinity and a mentor named Morpheus to join a rebellion against the Artificial Intelligences that have taken over planet earth. Morpheus believes that Neo is the One who will show people the way to freedom. Neo is set free from the Matrix, which is a computer-generated fantasy world designed to keep humans happy while they supply energy for the Artificial Intelligences. Once out of the Matrix, those who are free have the ability to return to the Matrix by hooking up with the Matrix computer. Their bodies remain free, but their minds enter the computer program and battle the representatives of Artificial Intelligence, the agents.

Toward the end of the movie, Neo, who has returned to the Matrix, is shot repeatedly by the most powerful agent, Mr. Smith. He bleeds and dies in the Matrix. Though only his mind is there, and his body is elsewhere, he still dies, convinced by his mind that he has been shot dead. Mr. Smith quips, "Goodbye, Mr. Anderson." But back on the ship, where Neo's body lies, Trinity looks at Neo lying there dead, and she starts talking quietly but earnestly. "Neo, I'm not afraid anymore. The Oracle told me that I would fall in love, and that the man I loved would be the One. So you see. You can't be dead. You can't be. Because I love you. You hear me? I love you."

She kisses him. And he comes alive again. He breathes.

Trinity tells him to get up. And back in the Matrix, he rises. The agents see him. They fire their guns, and he raises his hand and stops the bullets in their tracks. The bullets drop harmlessly to the floor. Neo attacks Agent Smith, enters his body and destroys him; the other agents run to escape. Neo leaves the Matrix. When he again returns to the Matrix with his mind, he is no longer controlled by the rules of the Matrix. Having returned from death, he can now show all the people a "world without rules and controls, without borders or boundaries. A world where anything is possible."

Neo comes back to life through the power of Trinity's love and the power of mind over matter.

■ *Do you think there is life after death? If so, what do you think it is like?*

■ *What do you think of the stories of people who say they died and then came back to life?*

Going Deeper

Have you ever experienced the death of someone close to you? The grief can be very painful and devastating. If it's a spouse, a son, a daughter or a parent, the grief and loss can sometimes last a lifetime and never seem to lift.

Death is the final frontier. What lies beyond death?

When we face death, we can resonate with the description in the Bible that death is the final enemy. Death seems to point to the absence of God as much as any experience we have in life. For the atheist, death is a cliff with no bottom.

And yet, death is also a time when we desperately need comfort and hope. Will we ever see our loved ones again? In the face of death, we often turn toward God. For only God knows (assuming God exists) what really is on the other side of the final frontier. And only God can reassure our hearts and give us hope for a springtime to come.

Is there life after death? Many people have reported near-death and after-death experiences. But those experiences, though interesting, are inconclusive because those people were resuscitated and then died again.

But what if someone came back from the dead and didn't die again? Now that would be news, wouldn't it? That would be something to pay attention to.

User's Guide

Paul shares his heart and the core of his faith with us in this writing. He is fighting people who had the conviction that life ends with death and that there is nothing after. He offers what he considers conclusive evidence that God is real, that faith is reasonable and that hope in life after death will be fulfilled. Look at his evidence, and then decide for yourself.

The Oracle

Now I would remind you, brothers and sisters, of the good news that I proclaimed to you, which you in turn received, in which you also stand, through which also you are being saved, if you hold firmly to the message that I proclaimed to you—unless you have come to believe in vain.

For I handed on to you as of first importance what I in turn had received: that Christ died for our sins in accordance with the scriptures, and that he was buried, and that he was raised on the third day in accordance with scriptures, and that he appeared to Cephas, then to the twelve. Then he appeared to more than five hundred brothers and sisters at one time, most of whom are still alive, though some have died. Then he appeared to James, then to all the apostles. Last of all, as to one untimely born, he appeared also to me. For I am the least of the apostles, unfit to be called an apostle, because I persecuted the church of God. But by the grace of God, I am what I am, and his grace toward me has not been in vain. On the contrary, I worked harder than any of them—though it was not I, but the grace of God that is with me. Whether then it was I or they, so we proclaim and so you have come to believe.

Now if Christ is proclaimed as raised from the dead, how can some of you say there is no resurrection from the dead? If there is no resurrection of the dead, then Christ has not been raised; and if Christ has not been raised, then our proclamation has been in vain and your faith has been in vain. We are even found to be misrepresenting God, because we testified of God that he raised Christ—whom he did not raise if it is true that the dead are not raised. For if the dead are not raised, then Christ has not been raised. If Christ has not been raised, your faith is futile and you are still in your sins. Then those also who have died in Christ have perished. If for this life only we have hoped in Christ, we are of all people most to be pitied.

But in fact Christ has been raised from the dead, the first fruits of those who have died. (1 Corinthians 15:1-20)

If the dead are not raised,

"Let us eat and drink,

for tomorrow we die." (1 Corinthians 15:32)

Musing

1. Paul claims that the resurrection of Christ is news based on evidence, not just a religious idea based on faith. What do you think of Paul's claim?
2. If this event happened today, what newspaper would report it, and on what page?
3. What's the evidence Paul gives that Jesus rose from the dead, and how strong do you think it is?
4. What holes in the evidence do you see?
5. What difference might the resurrection make to you when you face death?
6. What difference might the resurrection make in how we live in the here and now? (See the last line from 1 Corinthians 15:32.)
7. How might knowing that Jesus is very much alive today and has the power to overcome death help you in your journey to find God?

Challenge

Early Christians lived or died by one simple message: Jesus was alive. Jesus rose from the dead. That proved that he was God's Son, that God's power was with him, that he was innocent and that he took our sins on himself at the cross. He's alive! And that makes all the difference. We don't have to fear death. We can look forward to being reunited with all of our loved ones who follow Jesus. Jesus is here to talk to and walk with and be healed by in the here and now, because Jesus is alive!

So we have a choice. Will we put our trust in Jesus who rose from the dead—trust him with our life and our death and our hopes and our fears? Or will we turn away from eternal hope and just eat, drink and be merry, for tomorrow we die?

■ *How do you respond to this challenge?*

GOD MOMENT

Debbie's Story (told by Rick)

Debbie was interested in spiritual things, but she felt Christian faith was a crutch for mindless people. Yet she didn't think I was mindless. She just couldn't figure out how I could swallow that religious stuff.

I said I had good evidence for my faith, and she shot back, "Prove it!"

I replied, "Well, I could talk about evidence that makes God's existence likely or evidence that supports the reliability of the Bible. But here's the stuff that got to me. There is great evidence that Jesus came back to life from the dead and that he lives today to have a relationship with me."

"No way! What was it?"

"Here's the heart of it. The followers of Jesus turned the Roman world upside down based on one simple message, 'Jesus was dead and now he's alive.' Now, I wasn't there. But they were. They were in a position to know beyond a shadow of doubt whether that message was true or not."

"Wait a minute. Maybe they saw what they wanted to see," she challenged.

"But look here," I came back at her, and I showed her 1 Corinthians 15. "Over five hundred people at one time saw Jesus after he came back from the dead. And they were still around to confirm or deny the truth of the simple message." Then I showed her the story of Thomas, who had to see and touch to believe.

"Okay," she admitted. "So there's more to it than just the wishful thinking or hallucinations of a few people. Maybe they plotted it. They'd lost their leader and their power. So they stole the body and claimed he was still around."

38

"Good thought," I replied, "but not good enough!" (By that time we had a pretty good relationship.) "These people died for that simple message. People will preach a lie. But will they die for a lie? Ten of the twelve main followers of Jesus died a painful death because of their message. No way would they do that if their message was false and they knew it."

Debbie continued to grill me. She squirmed, and she came up with every possible alternative explanation. We looked at the theory that Jesus didn't die but only passed out. We looked at the idea that maybe the Romans stole the body, or maybe the Jews stole it. In the end, she recognized that the life of those early followers of Jesus just couldn't be explained in any better way. Jesus must have come back from the dead!

"Does anybody else know about this?" she asked, somewhat naively. "If this is true, this is big news! We have to get this out! Can we share this with some of my friends?"

"Well, sure," I responded.

That next week I returned to find a full dorm room. Debbie had invited all the students from her floor, and also all the other resident house fellows in the dorm, to hear the evidence for Jesus' coming back from the dead and being alive!

39

■ *In what ways does this story challenge your thinking?*

Self-Reflection

■ *Look back again at the spiritual journey spectrum you looked at in the first discussion. Where are you now, and have you moved? Why or why not?*

Skeptical   Apathetic   Curious   Actively Seeking   Feeling Connected   Following God

■ *What have you realized about yourself in this study?*

If you're comfortable, end with the following prayer: *God, thank you for raising Jesus from death. Thank you that Jesus is alive and is able to give me life. Jesus, I want to know you. I ask you to come into my life, and I commit myself to you as my forgiver, healer and leader.*

41

SIX

WHAT HAPPENS AFTER I FIND GOD?

Being a Christian is not just a good way to die, it's the best way to live.

BILL HYBELS

In the movie *Ace Ventura: When Nature Calls,* Ace, played by Jim Carrey, is a pet detective who solves cases of missing animals. As the movie opens, Ace tries to save a raccoon and fails. The raccoon slips out of Ace's hand to fall to its death thousands of feet below. Ace is devastated and joins a monastery. A man named Fulton seeks him out, finds him surrounded by animals, with butterflies fluttering about his head, and invites him to take a case, offering him a handsome rate of pay. Ace responds, "I am now a child of light. Your earthly money holds no appeal to me."

Fulton emphatically responds, "$20,000."

Ace hyperventilates, but then he says, "I cannot, for I am sorely needed here at the ashram."

Just then the head monk, who clearly wants Ace to leave, bursts in the door and points out that Ace is needed elsewhere and must go. Ace objects, "But I am yet to attain omnipresent supergalactic oneness."

The monk chimes in, "No, wait. There it is. You've just attained it."

Ace asks, "I have?"

The head monk responds, "Yes. Just now. You are one. I can see it in your eyes. You are more one than anyone."

Still skeptical, Ace asks, "But what about my medallion of spiritual accomplishment?"

The monk grabs his own and offers it: "Take mine."

Surprised, Ace comments, "But this took you eighty years to attain."

The monk replies, "That's okay. I don't like it anymore. Really."

Ace responds, "In the light of this personal sacrifice you've made, I have no choice but to take the case."

"Great!" exclaims the head monk. "I'll go tell the others."

Ace encourages the head monk, "Master, break it to them gently." As Ace leaves, the monks have a total off-the-chart party. They are laughing, somersaulting, drinking, yelling and celebrating, with balloons flying and party favors blaring. Ace comments on how sad denial is.

The scene is funny, as the monks are hysterically happy to get rid of Ace, and Ace is totally unaware of their true attitude. But the scene also represents a picture some of us might have of what happens when people get religious. They get a little weird, or even a lot weird.

■ *What's your picture of a person who is totally dedicated to God?*

■ *Can you relate to that picture, or are you put off by it?*

Going Deeper

Have you found God? Have you asked God to be your forgiver and healer and leader?

If so, you will want to know how to experience that new life, that transformation that God wants to give you. How do you experience life transformation? How do you experience that fresh start and that life as a new creation? Is it normal to be devoted to God, or is it a little weird?

We may have fears about our new commitment to God too. Is this a phase? Did anything really happen to me when I committed myself to become a Christ-follower? What difference will it really make? Is God going to ask me to do lots of things I don't want to do or feel unable to do? What happens next?

If you are still searching and haven't yet committed yourself to being a Christ-follower, you may still want to know what that would look like. How might you experience a fresh start and transformation if you became a Christ-follower?

User's Guide

Paul often explored great ideas. But he always brought them down to real life. In his various letters to people who had found God, he would start with these amazing and deep ideas, but then he would spend about half his time talking about how to live as a result of these challenging new ideas. Today we'll look at Paul's practical instructions on the new way to live and how that new way is even possible.

The Oracle

I pray that, according to the riches of his glory, he may grant that you may be strengthened in your inner being with power through his Spirit, and that Christ may dwell in your hearts through faith, as you are rooted and grounded in love. (Ephesians 3:16-17)

Put to death, therefore, whatever in you is earthly: fornication, impurity, passion, evil desire, and greed (which is idolatry). On account of these the wrath of God is coming on those who are disobedient. These are the ways you once followed, when you were living that life. But now you must get rid of all such things—anger, wrath, malice, slander, and abusive language from your mouth. Do not lie to one another, seeing that you have stripped off the old self with its practices and have clothed yourselves with the new self, which is being renewed in knowledge according to the image of its creator. In that renewal there is no longer Greek or Jew, circumcised and uncircumcised, barbarian, Scythian, slave and free; but Christ is all and in all!

As God's chosen ones, holy and beloved, clothe yourselves with compassion, kindness, humility, meekness, and patience. Bear with one another and, if anyone has a complaint against another, forgive each other; just as the Lord has forgiven you, so you also must forgive. Above all, clothe yourselves with love, which binds everything together in perfect harmony. And let the peace of Christ rule in your hearts, to which indeed you were called to one body. And be thankful. Let the word of Christ dwell in you richly; teach and admonish one another in all wisdom; and with gratitude in your hearts sing psalms, hymns, and spiritual songs to God. And whatever you do, in word or deed, do everything in the name of the Lord Jesus, giving thanks to God the Father through him. (Colossians 3:5-17)

Musing

1. In his prayer in the Ephesians passage, Paul first talks about where the power to live a new life comes from. What difference might it make to you that God can live in you by his Spirit, that the very power and presence of God are available to you when you become a Christ-follower?

2. Paul then talks about some things that we need to turn away from and not practice anymore. Which things hit you?

3. Paul is talking a lot about our relationships with others. Is there a hard or strained relationship that God may want you to work on? What step could you take?

4. What implications does Paul's thinking have for racism and prejudice, and why?

5. Why do you think forgiving others is so important?

6. Look at the final paragraph of the Oracle. Why do you think it may be important to let the word of Christ dwell richly in our hearts, and how might we do that?

7. Why do you think it may be important to participate in worship of God with others, and how might that happen for you?

8. What might it mean to do everything in the name of the Lord Jesus? Is that really a practical or attainable idea?

Challenge

You can't live for God on your own strength. But there's great news. You don't have to! When you ask God to be your forgiver and leader, God gives you his Spirit. God makes his home in you. That's why Paul can pray that God would strengthen us by his Spirit in our inner being. God's Spirit is there to give you the power to live a new life.

This new life includes things we turn away from, like destructive anger, self-centered sex, racial prejudice and greed. It also includes things we turn toward, like forgiving people who have hurt us, seeking their best, reading and learning God's Word, and worshiping with other Christians who can encourage us. We also seek to live for Jesus in front of others, and we carry a special concern for those who aren't yet in God's family. We can start expressing our caring for people still outside God's family by telling someone who is far from God how we have found God.

As we spend time with God and with others who have found God, we are strengthened in our inner being to live for God.

So we have a choice. Will we spend time with God in prayer and in reading the Bible? Will we spend time with others who know God? Will we live for God? Or will we try to do it alone—and gradually lose the sense of connection, encouragement and presence that God wants to give us?

■ *How do you respond to this challenge?*

GOD MOMENT

Abner's Story (continued from session three)

After telling Doug that God had better show up in my life over the next few days, I began to experience a sense of Jesus' presence everywhere I went. But that weekend I partied with my friends. I woke up Monday morning having thrown up, feeling hung over and miserable. I saw my life just going down the drain. I turned back to God.

That next Friday, I walked into my friend's room carrying my bong (my special marijuana pipe). My friends all looked up and smiled, ready for me to light up and get high with them. I did light up. I lit the whole thing on fire and burned it. My friends were shocked. "What are you doing?" they asked.

I told them, "I'm burning something I really love for something I love even more. I've committed myself to God." They were blown away. I was blown away. Now I'm hanging out with all these "crazy Christians," and I'm one of them!

■ *In what ways does this story speak to your life?*

Self-Reflection

■ *What have you realized about yourself in this study? What might you need to give up or turn away from in order to live for God? What might you most need to start doing in order to live for God?*

47

If you're comfortable, end with the following prayer: *God, help me to know you and be filled with your Spirit. Strengthen me in my inner being to love you, to love others and to live for you. God, I commit myself to following your leadership in my life and to seeking to live in your strength.*

LEADING A GIG

You have decided to help others enter into investigating God. Welcome to a great adventure! The following notes will help you use this guide to facilitate excellent spiritual discussions with others.

The first step is inviting another person or persons to join you for these discussions. You can get a lot of help in this process by ordering *The GIG Guide*, a training guide that teaches you how to pray, invite, prepare and lead these kinds of discussions. You can get it from the books area of the InterVarsity Christian Fellowship webstore <www.ivcf.org/store> or by calling toll-free 1-866-265-4823.

Once you have found someone who wants to join you, you can begin preparing to lead the discussion. You don't need to be an expert or know lots about the Bible to lead the discussion. You only need to be willing to learn and grow yourself, and to serve others in their spiritual journey.

Getting Started

Here are some tips to help you lead the first discussion.

1. Be ready to share your excitement. As you prepare, think through why you are interested in this particular discussion and theme. Your excitement will help people enter in. But make sure to share what *you* personally hope to learn from the discussion, not what you hope *they* learn. Remember, your goal is not to "preach" your point of view but to facilitate a helpful discussion on important spiritual issues. I have found that when I have this kind of attitude, I leave a lot of room for others to find their own way and for God to work in all of our lives.

2. Think about how to make everyone feel comfortable. Find a convenient location for conversation. Arrange the seating so you can see everyone and they can see each other. Provide food and drinks if you wish. Buy guides for each potential participant so that they can follow along. You can ask them to pay you back if they want to keep the guide.

3. Make sure everyone has met each other. You might want to use an icebreaker

question to get people talking. You can find ideas at InterVarsity Press's Small Group Center: <www.ivpress.com/smallgroups/smallgroupidea>.

4. Read over the series introduction. In your first session, you will need to summarize what is in the guide. Put it in your own words, but try to stick to the ideas that are there. It is very important for people to get a sense that these discussions and conversations are for them and their search, and not just a chance for you to convince them of your point of view. So anything is fair game, any opinion is welcomed, and any question is good. Challenge them to make the discussion work for where they are at. And if something isn't helping, encourage them to speak up about it. Read the discussion guidelines in the series introduction. Those guidelines can be very helpful!

5. After you have summarized the overall purpose of the series, you can have the participants read the first part of the introduction that describes this particular guide. This orients everybody to the theme of the guide; it's more effective to read it than just summarize it. Be sensitive to slow readers. You may want to have someone (or yourself) read it aloud. It will help people feel more comfortable if you say something like, "We're reading the introduction just to get us all on the same page and to get us intrigued with what we'll be talking about." At the end, you can ask if people are intrigued.

6. Be aware of the discussion dynamics in your group. They will change depending on the number of people you have. If you have several people coming, your challenges will be helping everyone participate and making sure no one dominates. You can help people by affirming quieter people when they share and talking with dominant ones outside the group. Encourage dominant ones to join you in helping others express their opinions. If you have only one other person in your group, the dynamics are different. You will ask questions and then let the conversation go back and forth between you, sharing honestly. You become both a leader and a group participant at the same time! Either situation, we've found, can work very well.

How to Lead a Session

Prepare for each session by going through the discussion by yourself. Let it affect your life. Make notes on what is hitting you, what is helpful, how you are struggling, what questions you have and what difference the study is making in your life.

After you have gone through the study yourself, look again at the "Challenge." That segment provides the main point of the discussion. Write out in your own words summaries of the written sections that you will not be reading aloud during the discussion. Read through this study's section of the leader's notes. There you will find details about how each session will work.

You'll also find information in the leader's notes about how to cue your VCR for the video clips in the introductions. All the times given for the movie clips are for the videocassette version (VCR) that you can rent at any local video rental place. So the times include the previews. If you rent the DVD version, the times given in the guide will be a little high, because the DVD version doesn't include previews in the movie segment. Be sure the video is set at the right spot ahead of time.

In each session, you will need to choose which sections to read to the group and which to have the group read. Generally, you'll just want to have the group read a couple sections along with the Scripture passage. All other sections should be summarized by you or put in your own words. Otherwise the discussion may become too tied to the guide and be less dynamic.

1. *Introduction.* Some sessions begin with movie clips. This can be an engaging way to start the session and get the group's attention. Show the clip, and then ask the questions in that section. (You won't need to use the written introduction.) Remember, however, that the clips are simply meant to get people talking. Don't get sidetracked by overanalyzing the movie and its interpretation. It should not take you more than fifteen minutes to watch the clip and discuss the question.

If there is no clip, then you or another group member should read the introductory paragraphs aloud, and then you can ask the questions provided. This portion of the study is important in helping people open up to the topic. Some will be intimidated by the idea of Scripture study, and these general questions may help them begin to feel comfortable.

2. *Going Deeper.* Next summarize both the "Going Deeper" and the "User's Guide" sections.

3. *The Oracle.* It is generally most effective to have people read "The Oracle" section silently.

4. *Musing.* Depending on your experience and comfort level, you might use these questions as they are or put them in your own words. If you do reword them, be careful not to create "yes or no" questions; they will not foster discussion.

5. *Challenge.* After the discussion of the passage, summarize the challenge section, and ask for the group's response. The challenge is the main point of the study and should provide an overall focus for you as you prepare and lead.

6. *God Moment.* Allow a few moments of silence to have the group read "God Moment," or read it aloud if there is enough time left.

7. *Self-Reflection.* Summarize the "Self-Reflection" and simple prayer parts, and give the group a minute of quiet to think or to pray in their hearts if they want to. If you are studying one on one, then don't have a quiet reflection time, because it can feel awkward. Instead, summarize the "Self-Reflection" question and prayer, and ask if the person wants to respond.

Finally, end the discussion by introducing the theme for next time and telling people why you are excited about it.

Going Deeper

While you are encouraging others to talk, it is important for you to offer your own struggles and insights with honesty and vulnerability. Pick a couple of points during the study—once during the "Oracle" section and once during the "Challenge" or "God Moment" section—to speak about what you are learning and experiencing in your life.

Sometime after the fourth discussion and before the last one, take stock of yourself, and help others take stock of where they are at. It is helpful to meet one on one at that point. Use a tool like *Circles of Belonging* (InterVarsity Press) or another gospel outline to summarize the message of God's love, and ask how the person wants to respond to that message.

Contextualizing

The discussion dynamics and style that are most helpful for any group depend on the culture of the members of the group. We have found that the instructions for preparing and leading that we have given you above work well for many ethnically white, Asian and Native American groups. But be culturally sensitive. For Chinese Americans or Japanese Americans, a confrontational and highly personal approach might be uncomfortable.

African American, Latino American or Korean American participants, however, often appreciate a more passionate, direct and strongly led approach. In such a context, you probably would not want to read aloud any of the sections. This might seem insincere and artificial. Instead, you will want to summarize and passionately speak out your convictions and personal experiences all the way through, especially in the "Challenge" and "God Moment" sections.

Even if you are leading the group in a cultural context where you share more often and more passionately, make sure to include a couple of the "Musing" questions. Your aim is helping others with their journey. They will grow as they express their convictions and questions. And their answers will give you a good read on where they are coming from, so when you speak passionately you will be speaking to their situation.

So, on with the adventure! Have a blast.

52

SESSION-BY-SESSION NOTES

Session One. Relational Path: Can I Find God Through Relationships?
Romans 8:31-39.

Main point. Only Jesus offers a relationship that cannot fail. We want people to see both how powerful human love can be and how much more lasting and powerful God's love is.

Video clip cue. Start at 1 hour and 13 minutes into part two of the video version. Start with Rose looking up at the Statue of Liberty, just before the man asks her name. Go for 4 minutes until she drops the diamond into the sea, or 6 minutes until she ends up in Jack's arms on the *Titanic*.

General note. The notes for this first study are more extended and detailed to give you an idea of how to use the various sections of the study in a discussion.

Introduction. The purpose of the movie clips is to help people to connect with the key question the study poses and to help them see ways the culture is addressing the question. Sometimes the movie clip makes a point that is in line with a Christian view of an issue, and sometimes the movie clip makes a point that is in opposition to a Christian point of view. One goal of the series is to help people express their point of view without feeling judged, so seeing a movie clip that affirms their perspective can help validate a person's experience. People are more open to change and growth when they are accepted, so that's where these studies start.

The clip from *Titanic* is powerful. It engages people at a significant level immediately. You want to affirm Rose's experience that relationships can change our lives. But you also want to raise the question of whether this is reality. Is the picture of Jack and Rose's relationship an ideal picture that is not often matched in our experience? What do we do with the dissonance between our romantic ideal and our life experience of people and relationships that disappoint us?

Question 1. Be ready to share an experience you have had of being loved by another person in a way that influenced your life for the good.

Question 2. God gave us his Son, who is a constant advocate for us, prays for us and remains committed to us through every hard life experience we have. You may find people can't relate to the idea of an unseen, intangible God loving us in concrete ways. If people respond by saying they can't relate to these dimensions of God's love, validate how hard it can be to directly experience the love of an unseen person. But affirm how powerful that might be if we could.

Question 3. An alternate question would be, "Have you ever felt close to God, and if so, when, and what was that like?"

Question 5. Be ready to share how much you want to have Paul's perspective in hard times and yet how difficult it can be. In general, you help people most when you share in ways they can identify with. Then when it is time to challenge them, they will trust you and listen.

Challenge. Summarize the main point of the study by sharing how the passage challenges you personally. Then you can ask what the discussion has brought to mind for the group members.

God Moment. If there is time, have them read the story to themselves, and ask if and how they can relate. Often you won't have time to read the personal story. But you can strongly encourage them to read it later on their own. That's another reason why it's helpful for each person to have a guide.

The "God Moment" story gives you an example of the kind of story you could share out of your life at the end. If you do share a personal story, make sure to ask if they can relate to your experience, and give them time to respond.

Self-Reflection. If you have a large group, you will want to give them a short time of quiet to respond. Then you can ask if anyone wants to share what they are thinking about. If your group is very small and some trust has been built, look at the self-reflection section together. Let them know they don't have to answer aloud, but that if they want to, you would be glad to hear how they respond. If they will tell you what they are thinking in that section, you will find it to be the most valuable and helpful part of the whole study because they will be letting you know where they are in their spiritual journey at that moment in their lives.

Prayer. In general, it is better not to pray aloud at first in a group where people are in different places in their journey. So let them pray on their own if they want to. In later weeks, for instance in the fifth and sixth studies, you may want to pray aloud, and encourage folks to join in with you by praying silently as you pray aloud. In a later session, it may also be appropriate to pray a short prayer aloud for someone who is going through a hard time and gives you permission to pray for them. But keep prayers short, encouraging and simple so that people can see themselves praying the same kind of prayer.

Session Two. Nature Path: Can I Find God Through Nature?
Acts 17:22-31.

Main point. We can sense God's existence and some of God's power through nature, but we can't really know God intimately through nature alone. One key thing you want people to see is that if God has made them, they are accountable to God for their choices.

Video clip cue. The scene begins 1 hour and 15 minutes into the video version of the movie. Start where Luke is holding up Yoda and a couple of rocks. It goes for 5 minutes, to where Yoda quips, "That is why you fail."

Introduction. The *Star Wars* clip gives a view of God that is common in our culture. God is the consciousness of the universe, a Force that we can be in harmony with but that makes no demands on us. The point of showing the clip is to get people talking about what they think God is like. So the question about whether God is more like a force or more like a person is important. C. S. Lewis, a well-known Christian writer and professor at Cambridge University, wrote that these are the two main views throughout history of what God is like. Western and Middle Eastern religions have seen God as more like a person, and Eastern religions have seen God as more like a force.

Your goal here is not to convince folks of what they should believe, but only to get them talking and thinking about these different views. Some people in your group may say they think God is like both. Others may say that they think God is not like either one. Whatever they say, you can help direct them toward what Paul thinks.

Question 1. Many people pursue spirituality in a totally self-absorbed and even materialistic way. Being spiritual doesn't help them become better people or more other-centered. That kind of spiritual search may be attractive, but it is ultimately self-centered and self-defeating. That's certainly what Paul thought about the ways many Athenians were seeking God by worshiping objects of gold and silver.

Question 2. God is the Maker of the universe and the Creator of all people. God is closer to us than we are to ourselves. In God we have our very life. God wants to be thought of for who God is, not demeaned or ignored.

Question 4. Be ready to share honestly what strengthens and weakens your desire to know and believe in God. Make sure to share some of your struggles here. You might share about your desire to do whatever you want the way you want, or your struggle to feel God in your life at some of the hard points. It helps a lot to share a specific experience and not just a general feeling. When you share about what strengthens your desire, you may want to mention a human relationship that has helped you.

Question 6. Think of a change you made in your life as a result of realizing that you are accountable to God. Be sure to share how you realized it was better in the end for you to choose to let God into your life on this issue. If it fits, you could start by saying, "One of my big battles with God has been over the issue of . . ." and then share about your struggle to make the choice, and then how it turned out. Areas of struggle in your life may include relationships, sex or lifestyle issues— or any area it was hard to let God into.

Session Three. Morality Path: Can I Find God by Being a Good Person?
Romans 1:18-25.

Main point. We all have a "self" or "sin" problem. We are addicted to self-rule, self-gratification, self-promotion. In this discussion, you want people to understand and recognize their own sin or self problem.

Video clip cue. Start at 2 hours and 29 minutes into the video version of the movie. Start where Maximus is standing, seeing into the afterlife. Then Commodus pulls a dagger and attacks. Show it for 5 minutes to the end of the movie.

Introduction. Maximus is rewarded in the next life because he was a good person and had loving relationships with his family in this life. The movie affirms the basic cultural idea that we can have a good life in the afterlife because of what we do in this life. You are using the movie clip here to show an example of the way people in our culture look at this issue.

Question 1. People often have a very negative stereotype about the anger of God. In this question you are beginning to help people see the justice of God's anger.

Question 2. The lie is in thinking that it is wise to neglect God and adore things and people.

Question 3. People want to do whatever they want. They don't want to be accountable to a Supreme Being. When we worship things and people, we can still do whatever we want to do. We don't have to change our lives. We don't have to be accountable.

Question 6. See the "Challenge" section.

Session Four. Pain Path: Can I Find God Through My Pain?
2 Corinthians 5:14-21.

Main point. Through Jesus' suffering—through the cross of Christ—we find forgiveness from God and reconciliation with God and others. Your goal in this discussion is for people to understand what the cross does to solve the self or sin problem.

Video clip cue. Start at 2 hours and 9 minutes into the video version of the movie. Start with Pacino's question about guilt. Go for 2.5 minutes, until Pacino ends with "I'm peaking. It's my time now. Our time." Be advised that this movie is rated R.

Introduction. Much of the pain we experience is caused by ourselves or by others close to us. The movie portrays God as a sadist who enjoys our pain. That is not what we've been seeing in our discussions!

Question 1. We become a new creation; we get a fresh start!

Question 2. God made Jesus, who had no sin, to "become sin" and receive the judgment that we deserved. He was experiencing spiritual death, or separation from God, for us.

Questions 3-5. Be ready to share personally and vulnerably.

Vicki's Story. This story is very important and powerful for this session. Be sure to include it.

Session Five. Mortality Path: Will I Find God in Life After Death?

I Corinthians 15:1-20.

Main point. Jesus' resurrection really happened! And it proves that through God's power there is life with God forever after death. You want people to see some of the evidence for the resurrection of Jesus and some of the implications. Jesus is alive!

Video clip cue. The scene begins at 2 hours and 8 minutes into the video version. Go for 5 minutes to the end of the movie.

Introduction. A popular movie like *The Matrix* shows how much the issue of life after death is a concern for all of us of every generation. The purpose of the clip and the questions is just to get people talking about their ideas of life after death.

Musing. The questions focus on the evidence for the resurrection and its influence on our lives. Spend some time working through the passage and the story to get the evidence clear in your own mind. It's strong evidence! If you want to look into it even more before the discussion, read Josh McDowell's *More Than a Carpenter* or the booklet titled *Evidence for the Resurrection* (IVP).

Make sure to give people the opportunity to talk about their personal response.

Session Six. The Path of Life: What Happens After I Find God?

Colossians 3:5-17.

Main point. We can live an empowered and transformed life by staying connected to Jesus and to Jesus' people. In this discussion, you want people to get a clear idea of their next steps in becoming a follower of Jesus. If some of the people in your group are not at a point of wanting to follow Jesus, encourage them to enter into the study just to see what it might be like if they ever did.

Video clip cue. Start at 9 minutes (including the previews) into the video version. Start where the man is climbing the stairs. Go 6 minutes to where Ace walks out of the monastery.

Introduction. The clip gets people laughing, but it also helps people start to talk about their stereotypes of "being religious." By voicing their fears, people may become more open to taking the next step in their journey with God.

59

Question 1. It can be encouraging to realize that God makes his home in us and then helps change us from the inside out!

Questions 2-3. Share personally about these questions.

Question 5. You may want to share the negative effects you felt at a time when it was hard for you to forgive.

Challenge. Share what has most helped you grow in your spiritual journey with God and others.

Conclusion. Consider ending by praying aloud a short, caring prayer for each person. And then discuss whether you want to keep meeting as a group, and if so, what you want to discuss. You may find another guide in this series will fit where people are at and what they want to talk about. You may also want to give them the booklets *Circles of Belonging* and *My Heart—Christ's Home* as final gifts for their spiritual journey.

ACKNOWLEDGMENTS

I am grateful to the many partners, friends and coworkers who gave invaluable feedback in the preparation of this series. I am especially thankful to my seeking friends who always keep me honest.

I am also grateful to my editor, Cindy Bunch, who went above and beyond in the preparation of these guides. She not only edited them, but she fieldtested them, advocated for them and provided invaluable friendship and support along the way. Thanks also to Debbie Abbs, who provided research for many of the quotes I used.

I also want to thank Terry Erickson and Alec Hill in InterVarsity Christian Fellowship, Nancy Ortberg at Willow Creek Community Church and Doug Yonamine at the Willow Creek Association for their support of this project.

Rick Richardson

61

RESOURCES

Groups Investigating God® from InterVarsity Press

These guides are designed to provide a safe place to explore your ideas about God—whatever you believe. They are great for discussions with two or more people.

Finding God: How Can We Experience God? by Rick Richardson
There are lots of places to look for God—like relationships, nature, goodness and even our own pain. Sometimes we have the sense that God is real. But we can't quite get hold of it. And then we may wonder if God even wants to be found. This discussion guide explores various paths people have used to find God.

Following God: What Difference Does God Make? by Daniel Hill
Sometimes we try to separate our personal beliefs from our actions and choices. It's easier—and more fun. But eventually that way of life starts to feel hypocritical and dissatisfying. The sessions in this guide address real-life questions about what it means to follow God.

Sex: What's God Got to Do with It? by Rick Richardson
Perhaps you've thought or heard statements like these: "God doesn't like sex." "Christianity is sexually repressive and oppressive toward women and gays." Here's an opportunity to explore for yourself what the Bible actually says about sexuality.

Spirituality: What Does It Mean to Be Spiritual? by Rick Richardson
Many of us have tried various spiritual activities—meditation, nurturing our souls through listening to spiritual teachers, by reading books by those who seem to be ahead of us or by visiting church services or religious groups. Yet the search continues. And we feel empty. These sessions explore questions about finding spiritual satisfaction.

Other InterVarsity Press Resources

Circles of Belonging by Rick Richardson
A brief booklet offering a straightforward presentation of the message of Jesus that speaks deeply to the minds and hearts of people today.

Evangelism Outside the Box by Rick Richardson
If you are looking for ways to reach out to people and for help in responding to the new questions people are asking, this book will give you many helpful and practical ideas.

Jesus with Dirty Feet by Don Everts
An intriguing and compelling new look at Jesus that breaks through a lot of our stereotypes and misconceptions about who this man was and what he wanted.

My Heart—Christ's Home by Robert Boyd Munger
A booklet offering a simple, moving description of how we can make room in our hearts for God to become the center of our lives.

Other Resources

The Case for Christ and *The Case for Faith* by Lee Strobel
If you have tough questions about the rationality and credibility of Christian faith, these books are for you. Lee Strobel is a former atheist who looks at the questions that kept him from believing in God. Available from Zondervan Publishing.

GIG Training Guide
This guide to GIGs (Groups Investigating God) will give you immense help in starting and leading spiritual discussion groups for seekers. Available from InterVarsity Christian Fellowship at 1-866-265-4823 or <www.ivcf.org/store>.

Visit the InterVarsity Press website at <www.ivpress.com>.